KILLING TIME

Featuring WINWOOD AND CORD

MANDARIN

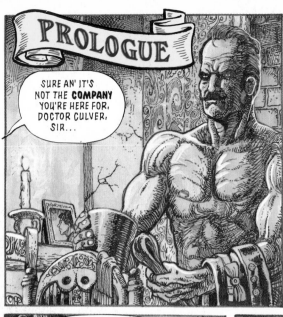

SURE AN' IT'S NOT THE **COMPANY** YOU'RE HERE FOR, DOCTOR CULVER, SIR...

A GIRL'S GOT TO BE CAREFUL OF A NIGHT.

WHY, YOU COULD BE **SAUCY JACK** HIMSELF, FOR ALL I KNOW...

NOW COME AN' SIT BY ME, OR YOU'LL HAVE ME THINKIN' YOU'RE **SHY**.

OH, AND WHAT'S THAT YOU'RE HIDING FROM ME NOW?

IS IT A **PRESENT** YOU'VE GOT THERE? A PRESENT FOR YOUR FALLEN ANGEL?

A PRESENT.

YES.

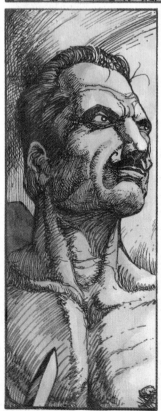

OH, **MURDER**!

WINWOOD AND CORD IN
AN INDIGO PRIME STORY
KILLING TIME
BY SMITH AND WESTON
PART: ONE

MURDER! MURDER!

WHITECHAPEL MURDER!

JACK THE RIPPER STRIKES AGAIN!

REOWRRR!

LONDON: NOVEMBER THE NINTH, 1888. SIX O'CLOCK ON THE DOT.

WE'RE HERE.

HE'S DONE IT AGAIN.

WHAT?

THE RIPPER.

OH, OUR DELIGHTFUL DOCTOR CULVER.

YES, THAT'D BE MARY JANE KELLY. HALF-THREE THIS MORNING. SHE'S BY FAR THE WORST ONE, AFTER MISS BOYD.

BUT THEN THAT HASN'T HAPPENED YET, HAS IT?

PROFESSOR Vernon Seward
MRIGB - ScD

WINWOOD AND CORD.

PROFESSOR SEWARD IS EXPECTING US.

OH, MY LORD...

WHAT A COLLECTION. THIS PLACE IS AMAZING... ABSOLUTELY AMAZING.

I BET IT NEEDS A LOT OF DUSTING.

CAN I HELP YOU AT ALL?

PROFESSOR SEWARD... PROFESSOR SEWARD, YOU HAVE MY DEEPEST CONGRATULATIONS.

I DON'T KNOW WHO THE DEVIL YOU ARE, SIR, BUT I'D APPRECIATE IT IF YOU LEFT MY HOUSE NOW.

I'M EXPECTING GUESTS FOR DINNER IN A SH—

MAX, WE DON'T GO GATECRASHING PARTIES WITHOUT AN INVITE. RULES OF THE HOUSE — REMEMBER?

I DON'T WANT TO SPEND THE NEXT FIVE HUNDRED YEARS CLEANING UP TEMPORAL ANOMALIES AFTER YOU.

OH, I'M MOST AWFULLY SORRY, OLD BOY. IT QUITE SLIPPED MY MIND.

WHAT...?

AHH, PROFESSOR.

YOU WERE SAYING SOMETHING ABOUT DINNER, I BELIEVE?

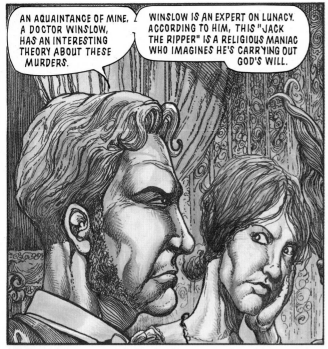

AN ACQUAINTANCE OF MINE, A DOCTOR WINSLOW, HAS AN INTERESTING THEORY ABOUT THESE MURDERS.

WINSLOW IS AN EXPERT ON LUNACY. ACCORDING TO HIM, THIS "JACK THE RIPPER" IS A RELIGIOUS MANIAC WHO IMAGINES HE'S CARRYING OUT GOD'S WILL.

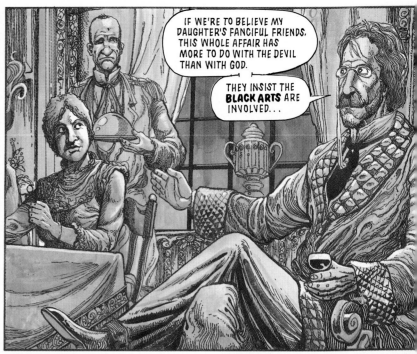

IF WE'RE TO BELIEVE MY DAUGHTER'S FANCIFUL FRIENDS, THIS WHOLE AFFAIR HAS MORE TO DO WITH THE DEVIL THAN WITH GOD.

THEY INSIST THE **BLACK ARTS** ARE INVOLVED...

WHEN IT COMES TO MATTERS OF THE SPIRIT WORLD, FATHER'S MIND IS FIRMLY CLOSED.

AND WHAT OF MISS MARGARET FOX, **SPIRITUALIST EXTRAORDINAIRE**? WHY, SHE HERSELF CONFESSED TO FRAUD NOT SIX MONTHS AGO.

NO, MARY. THE WORLD HAS SIMPLER SOLUTIONS.

OH, COME ON NOW, VERNON... EVEN **YOU** AREN'T AVERSE TO A LITTLE MYSTERY. WHAT ABOUT OUR PRESENCE HERE TONIGHT?

SIR CHARLES HAS A POINT. ARE YOU GOING TO TELL US WHAT THIS INVENTION OF YOURS **IS**, PROFESSOR?

YES, PROFESSOR. **DO** TELL US.

VERY WELL.

IF NONE OF THE LADIES HAVE ANY OBJECTION, PERHAPS WE COULD GO THROUGH TO THE SMOKING ROOM?

A Revelation

TONIGHT, BEFORE YOUR VERY EYES, I HOPE TO PROVIDE AN ANSWER TO THAT MOST ENDURING OF PHILOSOPHICAL QUESTIONS:

WHICH CAME FIRST? THE CHICKEN OR THE EGG?

ERE YOU HAVE IT, LADIES AND GENTLEMEN...

I THINK YOU'LL AGREE THAT THERE'S RESOUNDING EVIDENCE IN FAVOUR OF THE EGG.

THE JOURNAL OF PROFESSOR VERNON SEWARD...

10th November, 1888.

While Mary attended to the guests upstairs, I began a final series of checks on the machine.

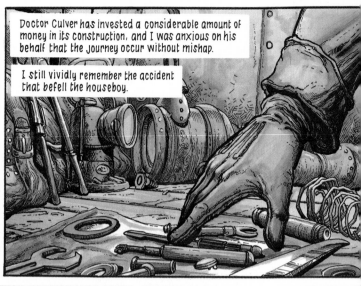

Doctor Culver has invested a considerable amount of money in its construction, and I was anxious on his behalf that the journey occur without mishap.

I still vividly remember the accident that befell the houseboy.

I told Mary I had dismissed him for over-familiarity with the parlourmaid, something she herself had remarked upon on numerous occasions.

I am only thankful he had no family.

Of more concern to me is the unexpected arrival of my old friend and sparring partner, Max Winwood. He has grown into the most peculiar fellow.

At times, he brings the memories of our years at Eton flooding back; at other times I am convinced he is a complete stranger.

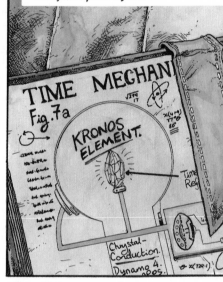

I was particularly suprised by the comment he m after the demonstration last night, regarding th "disharmonies in the resonance crystal!"

Winwood dismissed my praise, insisting that h was simply an interested amateur, but the remark showed a breadth of knowledge very nearly the equal of my own.

TIME MECHAN
Fig.7a

KRONOS ELEMENT.

Crystal-
Conduction.
Dynamo 4.

I must admit to some scepticism regarding his story of being a missionary in The Congo. I suspect that his arrival here belies some deeper motive.

Only time will tell.

IS ALL THIS TOMFOOLERY REALLY **NECESSARY**, SEWARD?

I'M AFRAID I'M IN AGREEMENT WITH YOU, MAJOR. THESE ENDLESS CHARADES ARE BECOMING MOST **FRIGHTFULLY** TIRESOME.

I THINK IT'S ABSOLUTELY **THRILLING**...

I IMAGINE YOU WOULD, DEAR.

I APOLOGISE FOR THE INCONVENIENCE Y HAVE ALL BEEN THROUGH, BUT I'M SURE YOU'LL FIND OUR ADVENTURE TODAY MOF THAN ADEQUATE RECOMPENSE...

IF FAT IS KIND, WE ARE ALL DESTINED TO BECON A PART OF HISTORY...

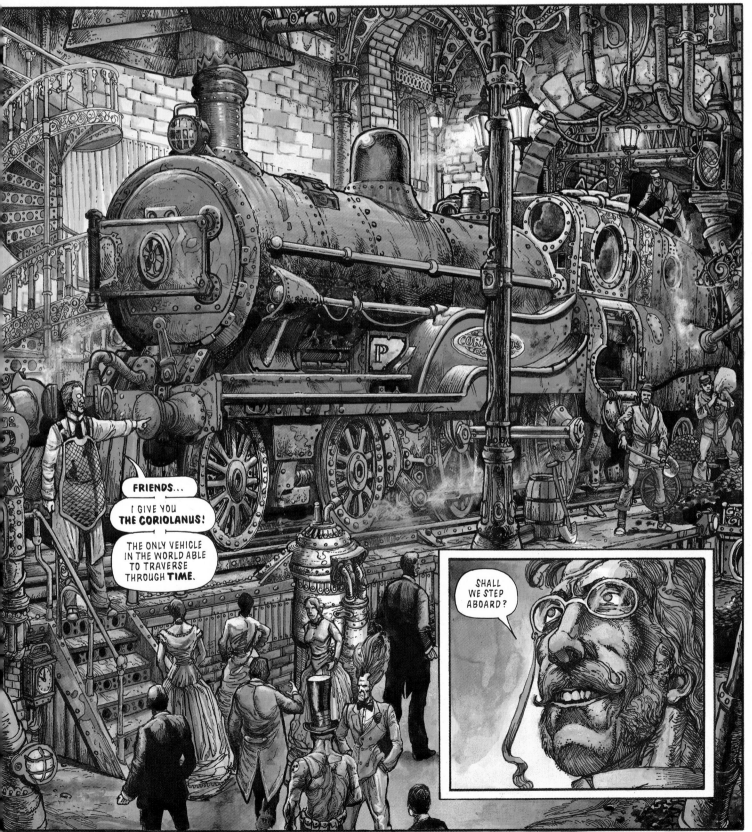

Miss Charlotte Boyd's First Impressions

"IMMEDIATELY BEHIND THE ENGINE ITSELF IS THE **CONSERVATORY**, A LIFE-LONG PASSION OF MINE..."

"IT BOASTS A SMALL BUT DIVERSE COLLECTION OF FLORA, INCLUDING SOME OF THE RAREST, MOST BEAUTIFUL PLANTS IN THE WORLD."

"OH, IT'S **WONDERFUL**. IT'S JUST LIKE THE GARDENS AT KEW, ISN'T IT, DONALD?"

"THE **SLEEPING** CAR..."

"UNFORTUNATELY, THE SHORTAGE OF CARRIAGES MEANS WE HAVE ONLY SIX ROOMS, INCLUDING LAVATORY AND BATHROOM, BUT WE HOPE TO ACCOMODATE EVERYONE WITH REASONABLE EASE.

"NEXT WE HAVE THE **DAY ROOM**..."

"IT WOULD HAVE BEEN UNSEEMLY TO INCLUDE A SMOKING ROOM AND IGNORE THE LADIES AMONGST US, SO WE SETTLED ON A COMPROMISE.

"NATURALLY THE ROOM COMES EQUIPPED WITH A WELL-STOCKED DRINKS CABINET...

"THE **PASSENGER COMPARTMENTS**...

"A RATHER ORDINARY BUT NEVERTHELESS IMPORTANT INCLUSION. AS WELL AS ENSURING SOME PRIVACY, THEY ALSO PROVIDE A VANTAGE POINT FROM WHICH TO VIEW THE SIGHTS.

"AND FINALLY, THE **DINING CAR**...

"THE REDOUBTABLE MRS HARRIS HAS VOLUNTEERED TO TRAVEL WITH US, SO WE NEED NONE OF US FACE THE AWFUL SPECTRE OF PICNIC HAMPERS AND COLD COLLATIONS.

"THE KITCHEN AND SERVANTS' QUARTERS ARE BOTH LOCATED IN THE END CARRIAGE."

IT'S ALL SO **GRAND**, PROFESSOR.

I DON'T THINK EVEN THE QUEEN **HERSELF** COULD FIND FAULT WITH ANYTHING HERE.

WE ARE HOPING VICTORIA AND ALBERT WILL GRACE US WITH THEIR PRESENCE ONCE WE'VE MADE PUBLIC OUR FINDINGS AND UNVEILED **THE CORIOLANUS**.

WHO'S "**WE**"?

ISHMAEL!

...MUST FORGIVE MY COMPANION'S ...NTNESS. HE'S HAD RATHER AN ...CONVENTIONAL UPBRINGING...

...RED BY NATIVES IN THE AFRICAN ...GLE. WE FOUND HIM FLOATING ...WN THE CONGO IN A TEA CHEST.

KIDNAPPED BY CANNIBALS, EH? POOR CHAP'S LUCKY TO BE ALIVE...

THERE REALLY IS NO DARK SECRET ABOUT THE MATTER, MR CORD. MY ASSOCIATE IS DOCTOR CULVER...

HE'S INVESTED A CONSIDERABLE SUM OF MONEY IN MY RESEARCH, AS WELL AS HELPING SOLVE SEVERAL **THORNY** MASS-TIME CALCULATIONS.

OH... I MUST'VE MADE A **MISTAKE**, THEN. I THOUGHT THE DOCTOR WAS ONLY QUALIFIED AS A PHYSICIAN...

...T'S TRUE. BUT I'M ALSO A MAN OF ...GRESSIVE VIEWS. THE TWO ...LOOKS ARE NOT INCOMPATIBLE.

MONTAGU WAS QUICK TO APPRECIATE THE IMPLICATIONS OF MY RESEARCH.

TEMPEROLOGY — AS I CALL THIS FIELD — OFFERS UNTOLD BENEFITS, NOT LEAST FOR THE MEDICAL PROFESSION.

IT SOUNDS SIMILAR TO THE HOT SPRINGS OF **BATH**. ALTHOUGH TREATMENT IS WONT TO BE LENGTHY, THE WATER HAS A MOST BENEFICIAL EFFECT IN CASES OF GOUT AND RHEUMATISM.

WHO **ARE** THOSE TWO FELLOWS?

I WAS SURPRISED TO SEE THEM AT DINNER LAST NIGHT, BUT I'D NO IDEA THEY WOULD BE COMING WITH US TODAY.

MAX IS...

MAX IS AN OLD FRIEND. WERE AT SCHOOL TOGETH I COULDN'T LET HIM MIS OUT ON OUR EXPEDITION.

WHERE EXACTLY **IS** OUR DESTINATION, PROFESSOR?

THE EARLY PALEOLITHIC, LADY JOCELYN. FORTY THOUSAND YEARS AGO.

SPEAKING OF WHICH...

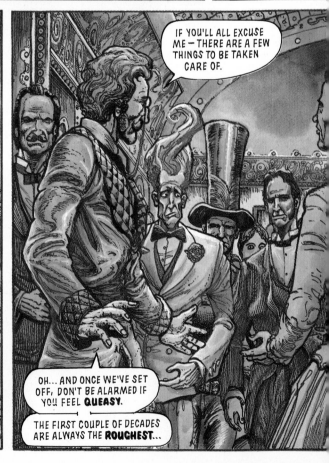

IF YOU'LL ALL EXCUSE ME — THERE ARE A FEW THINGS TO BE TAKEN CARE OF.

OH... AND ONCE WE'VE SET OFF, DON'T BE ALARMED IF YOU FEEL **QUEASY**.

THE FIRST COUPLE OF DECADES ARE ALWAYS THE **ROUGHEST**...

By two o'clock we had worked up a considerable head of steam — well over the 250 psi needed to achieve escape velocity — and we left the tunnel like a cork from a champagne bottle.

As we accelerated, I found myself thinking of the houses above us — the whole of Belgrave Sq — indeed the whole of London — blissfully unaware of what was happening beneath their very feet.

Then, the Kronos element was suddenly vitalised, and all thought left me as The Coriolanus slid sideways out of time.

The effects caused by the initial displacement, are short-lived but very disturbing.

A strange quality of elasticity is imparted to the very air around one, and one feels light-headed — a sensation almost like intoxication.

There is also a considerable build-up of electrical charge, often enough to set the whole of the locomotive alight with St Elmo's fire.

It is, however, in the joints that I am most affected. They are wracked by an interminable pain, like tuning forks struck by a hammer.

I must remember to ask Culver if the phenomenon has any medical basis.

Once we were set firmly upon our course, I joined the others in the day car.

They seemed for the most part stunned. Even Lady Jocelyn, usually the most loquacious of women, was lost for words (which is, in itself, an historic event).

I could not help but wonder what the future held in store for us.

DO YOU REALLY THINK WE SHOULD HAVE LET LYTTELTON GO **OFF** LIKE THAT...? I CAN'T SEE THE NATIVES TAKING KINDLY TO AN OLD SOLDIER WITH A **BLUNDERBUSS**...

THE MAJOR IS AN ENGLISHMAN, MR MAYBURY. THE ENGLISH HAVE ALWAYS BEHAVED **IMPECCABLY** WHEN ABROAD.

BUT DOES THE SAME RULE APPLY IN THE EARLY **STONE AGE**, LADY JOCELYN?

EVEN MORE SO.

HAVE YOU CONSIDERED THE POSSIBILITY OF A DOMINO EFFECT? THAT DAMAGE INCURRED HERE MIGHT ACTUALLY AFFECT THE **FUTURE**?

ECHO **BACK**, AS IT WERE.

YOU COULD CAUS— SOME VERY NAST— ≷ BHURRP ≷ SCREW-UPS.

WOULD ANYONE CARE FOR ANOTHER SANDWICH?

LADY JOCELYN?

NOT FOR ME, MY DEAR, THANK YOU ALL THE SAME.

I'VE HAD AN AVERSION TO SHELLFISH EVER SINCE I ATE SOME **FOUL** LOBSTER AT THE QUEEN'S JUBILEE LAST —

BOOOOM!

KILLING TIME

WINWOOD AND CORD IN — AN INDIGO PRIME STORY

BY SMITH AND WESTON — PART: THREE

A Day in the Country

THE SCOUNDREL CAME RUNNING AT ME OUT OF THE TREES. HOLLERED LIKE A BALLY **MADMAN.**

STILL, I BAGGED THE FELLOW.

NASTY HOLE IN THE CHEST, BUT THE HEAD'S UNMARKED.

SHOULD LOOK **SPLENDID** ON THE DRAWING ROOM WALL, EH?

On Evolution and the Monarchy

IT GOES **BEYOND** THAT, CHARLES...

NATURAL SELECTION ISN'T JUST A BIOLOGICAL PROCESS. IT'S THE DRIVING FORCE BEHIND OUR WHOLE EVOLUTION.

CULTURE, INDUSTRY, ART...

MY DEAR CHAP, I DON'T DISPUTE THE FACT FOR A MOMENT.

BUT YOU MUST ADMIT THAT FINDING OUT ONE'S DESCENDED FROM **APES** IS FAR FROM FLATTERING.

I DREAD TO THINK WHAT WILL HAPPEN WHEN THE COLONIES LEARN THAT THE HEAD OF THE BRITISH EMPIRE IS A HIGHLY-EVOLVED **MONKEY**.

BUT WE HAVE THE **EVIDENCE**, CHARLES. OUR **NEANDERTHAL** FRIEND IS ALL WE **NEED**.

WHEN WE TAKE HIM BACK TO LONDON, THEY'LL **HAVE** TO BELIEVE. DARWIN WILL FINALLY BE VINDICATED...

THEN WHY CONTINUE WITH OUR JOURNEY?

IF YOU HAVE WHAT YOU CAME FOR, WHY GO ON?

TO **LEARN**, CHARLES. TO FIND OUT **MORE**.

EVEN A SCEPTIC LIKE YOURSELF MUST BE CURIOUS ABOUT HIS ORIGINS.

WAIT UNTIL YOU **SEE** IT, CHARLES...

THE FIRST AMPHIBIANS CRAWLING FROM THE WAVES AND HEAVING THEMSELVES ONTO DRY LAND... THAT'LL BE A SIGHT TO TAKE TO YOUR GRAVE.

EXCUSE ME INTERRUPTING, PROFESSOR, BUT MARY IS HOLDING A **SEANCE** IN THE DAY ROOM...

WE WERE WONDERING IF YOU'D LIKE TO ATTEND, SIR CHARLES?

I'M SORRY, MY DEAR, BUT I'M AFRAID I'M FAR TOO **WORLDLY-MINDED** TO BE OF ANY VALUE TO YOU.

BESIDES WHICH, OUR HOST HAS JUST BEEN EXPLAINING TO ME HOW WE ARE ALL DESCENDED FROM **APES**...

...AND I'M NOT SURE THAT APES **HAVE** SOULS.

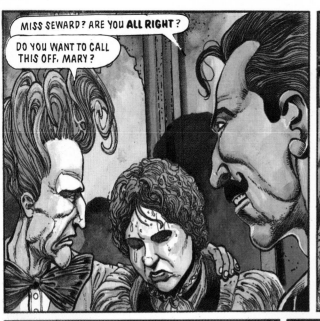

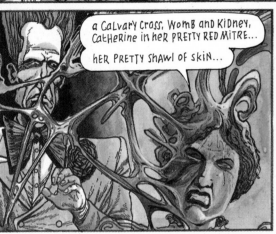

EEEEEEAAH

THAT SOUNDED LIKE **MISS BOYD**...

I KNEW IT.

I **KNEW** IT!

LANGHAM...

WHAT THE **DEUCE** IS GOING ON, MAN?

IT'S THE OTHERS. MARY AND THE OTHERS. THEY WERE HOLDING A **SEANCE** AND...

I THINK SOMETHING'S GONE WRO

WINWOOD AND CORD IN
KILLING TIME
AN INDIGO PRIME STORY
BY SMITH AND WESTON
PART: FOUR

Help is Administered

I'LL BRING THE GUN.

I'VE HEARD SOME QUEER STORIES ABOUT THE **DEVILS** THAT CAN BE DRAGGED UP AT THESE THINGS.

LET'S SEE HOW THEY STAND UP TO A BELLYFUL OF **LEAD**...

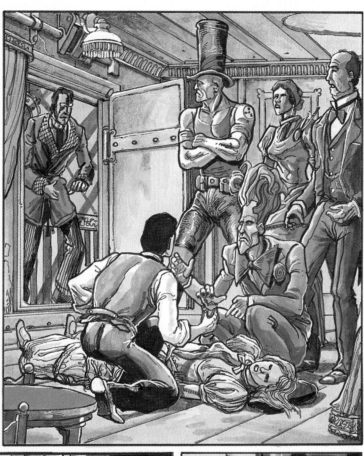

H, THANK **HEAVENS** YOU'RE ERE, PROFESSOR... WE WERE LL QUITE AT A **LOSS** AS TO WHAT WE SHOULD DO.

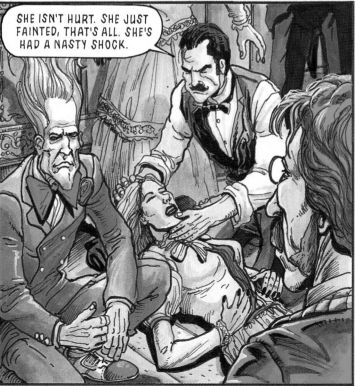

SHE ISN'T HURT. SHE JUST FAINTED, THAT'S ALL. SHE'S HAD A NASTY SHOCK.

WHAT HAPPENED?

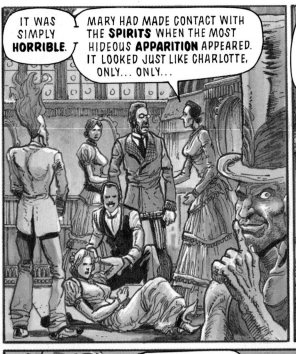

IT WAS SIMPLY **HORRIBLE**.

MARY HAD MADE CONTACT WITH THE **SPIRITS** WHEN THE MOST HIDEOUS **APPARITION** APPEARED. IT LOOKED JUST LIKE CHARLOTTE, ONLY... ONLY...

IT WAS PROBABLY JUST SOME FREAK **ECTOPLASMIC MATERIALISATION**, THAT'S ALL. I IMAGINE TRAVELLING THROUGH TIME CAUSES THESE KIND OF **ANOMALIES**.

NOT THAT I'M ANY **EXPERT**, OF COURSE.

I MADE A MISTAKE.

IS THAT WHAT YOU WANT ME TO SAY, FATHER? I MADE A MISTAKE. YOU WERE RIGHT AND I WAS WRONG.

BUT WE SHOULD NEVER HAVE COME ON THIS JOURNEY. THERE'S SOMETHING OUT THERE, AND IT **KNOWS** US...

SOMETHING **DID** HAPPEN, PROFESSOR. WE **ALL** FELT IT.

LADY JOCELYN...

I'M TRYING TO TALK TO MY DAUGHTER.

WHY DON'T YOU KEEP YOUR MOUTH **SHUT** FOR JUST A FEW MINUTES?

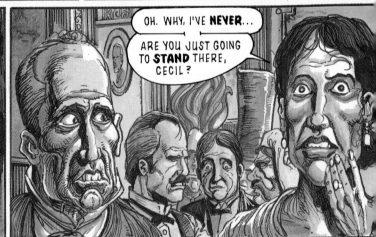

OH. WHY, I'VE **NEVER**...

ARE YOU JUST GOING TO **STAND** THERE, CECIL?

YOU DON'T **UNDERSTAND! NONE OF YOU UNDERSTAND!**

I **SAW** IT. THE CUTTING...THE HANDS, CUTTING INSIDE HER... DIVIDING HER UP...

IT'S OUT THERE, JUST WAITING...ALL THAT TWISTED, SCALDED FLESH, PATCHED WITH FACES...

AND THE **CHILDREN**...

LICKING IT, LICKING AWAY ALL THE BLOOD AND, AND...

SOMETHING'S GOING TO HAPPEN!

SOMETHING DREADFUL'S GOING TO HAPPEN!

I'M AFRA[I]D WE'RE GOING [TO] DIE...

SHE SAW IT, DIDN'T SHE? **THE ISCARIOT?**

I'M AFRAID SHE DID, YES. IT'S JUST OUR LUCK THERE HAPPENS TO BE A **MEDIUM** ON BOARD.

BUT DID YOU SEE THE **ECTOPLASM** SHE PRODUCED? THE FIGURE IT FORMED? NOW THAT, I THOUGHT, WAS A VERY CLEVER PIECE OF THEATRE... VERY **GRAND GUIGNOL**...

MEAN THE **PENTAGRAM**? THE WAY FIVE POINTS MARKED THE LOCATION **THE RIPPER** MURDERS? THAT, OF COURSE, BUT ALSO ITS **OCCULT** SIGNIFICANCE...

IT'S A SIGN OF **CONJURATION**. IT'S THE STAR WHICH LED **THE MAGI** TO THE INFANT **CHRIST**. WITH THE TWO POINTS IN THE ASCENDANT, IT'S THE SIGN OF **SATAN**.

OUR MISS SEWARD IS A VERY **ASTUTE** YOUNG LADY.

L, SHE DOESN'T SEEM TO HAVE TONED-ON ABOUT **CULVER** YET. UGH ONCE HE'S KILLED MISS D, THEY'RE GOING TO KNOW THE RIPPER SOON ENOUGH.

YOU MEAN WE'RE STILL GOING TO LET THAT HAPPEN? WE'RE GOING TO SIT HERE AND LET HIM CARVE HER UP LIKE SOME **SUNDAY JOINT**?

WE'VE NO **ALTERNATIVE**, OLD BOY. IT PAINS ME AS MUCH AS IT DOES YOU. BUT WHAT ELSE CAN WE DO?

MAX, I'VE BEEN THINKING...

WHY DON'T WE GO BACK TO **INDIGO PRIME**? GO STRAIGHT TO **VISTA**, PUT IN FOR A **RECURSION LOOP**... MAYBE EVEN GET **THE SCENESHIFTERS** TO REROUTE THE WHOLE **PARALLEL**?

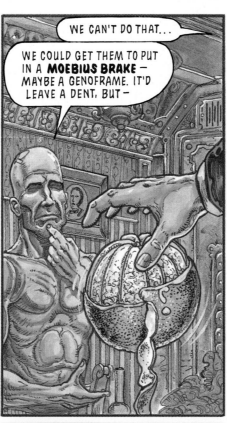

WE CAN'T DO THAT...

WE COULD GET THEM TO PUT IN A **MOEBIUS BRAKE** — MAYBE A **GENOFRAME**. IT'D LEAVE A DENT, BUT —

WE CAN'T DO THAT!

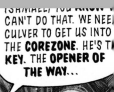

I5HMAEL, YOU KNOW CAN'T DO THAT. WE NEE CULVER TO GET US INTO THE **COREZONE**. HE'S T KEY. THE **OPENER OF THE WAY**...

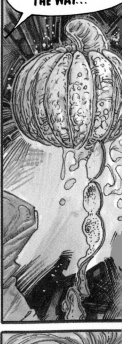

"IF WE STOP CULVER NOW, **THE ISCARIOT** IS JUST GOING TO KEEP ON **GROWING**... SHUFFLING PEOPLE AND PLACES AROUND UNTIL IT'S AMASSED ENOUGH ENERGY TO BREAK OUT.

"DO YOU REALLY **WANT** THAT, ISHMAEL? THE ISCARIOT MANIFEST IN **OUR** REALITY?

"DO YOU REMEMBER WHAT IT DID THE **LAST** TIME?"

AN HOUR, AND HE'LL HAVE STARTED ON CHARLOTTE.

WE'LL GIVE HIM, SAY, THREE HOURS TO FINISH CUTTING HER UP. THEN WE CAN MOVE IN.

AFTER THAT, OLD BO' YOU CAN DO WHATEVE YOU **WANT** TO HIM.

THAT'S A **PROMISE**.

IN TRANSIT

THE JOURNAL OF PROFESSOR VERNON SEWARD
11TH NOVEMBER, 1888

The day began favourably enough, but soon fell into disorder. Major Lyttleton was the cause of our first misfortune when he staged an impromtu one-man hunting expedition shortly after lunch. The only profitable result of this is that we now have a specimen of *Neanderthalensis*, albeit a dead one.

The cadaver has been packed in ice — it should cause great consternation upon our return.

The second mishap was the result of my daughter's attempt at making contact with the "spirit world." She certainly succeeded in *scaring* Miss Boyd — the poor woman was rendered senseless.

Mary insists that what occured was a warning of some terrible future event. But I'm afraid it shows she is still obsessed with an irrational desire to contact the spirit of her dead, demented mother.

I must dissuade Mary from such misguided conduct in the future. The atmosphere on the train has grown quite oppressive enough already.

The further back in time we go, the stronger it seems to become — a leaden pressure insinuating its way in from outside, darkening one's very thoughts.

Perhaps Sir Charles was right in questioning the outcome of the journey.

We are already some sixty-million years back in time. What awaits us if we continue even **further**?

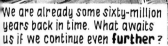

We are another day away from our journey's end. And, perhaps more dauntingly, the world's beginning.

Who knows what horrors might lie beyond **that**?

WINWOOD AND CORD IN

AN INDIGO PRIME STORY

KILLING TIME

BY SMITH AND WESTON

PART: FIVE

Decisions are Made

JUDAS.

YOU FEEL THAT? THE AIR PRESSURE JUST DROPPED AGAIN...

SHMAEL, WHY DON'T YOU SIT DOWN? WE CAN'T DO A THING UNTIL WE'RE IN THE **COREZONE**, SO YOU MIGHT AS WELL MAKE THE MOST OF THINGS.

I'M GOING TO FIND SEWARD.

IF ANY **SOMAFORMS** HAVE GOT IN FROM OUTSIDE, HE'S GOING TO NEED HELP SEALING OFF THE TRAIN...

LOOK, I KNOW HOW YOU FEEL, OLD BOY, BUT CULVER **HAS** TO KILL MISS BOYD.

IF HE DOESN'T OPEN THE THRESHOLD WE'LL NEVER MAKE IT THROUGH TO **THE ISCARIOT**. WE'LL JUST HAVE BEEN WASTING OUR TIME.

IF YOU WANT TO HELP SEWARD, FIRE AWAY. JUST LEAVE CULVER TO GET ON WITH IT, THERE'S A GOOD CHAP.

...CUTTING... HE'S C-C-CUTTING INSIDE ME... INSIDE MY B-B-B...

HUSH, CHARLOTTE. EVERYTHING WILL BE ALL RIGHT. YOU'LL SEE.

HUSH...

NOK-NOK

COME IN...

OH. DONALD. I DIDN'T REALISE YOU WERE STILL HERE. I THOUGHT, IN ALL THIS CONFUSION, MISS BOYD MIGHT HAVE BEEN LEFT ALONE.

WHAT CONFUSION?

YOU DIDN'T HEAR IT? ONE OF THE WINDOWS IN THE PASSENGER CAR BROKE. IT APPARENTLY CAUSED A LOT OF DAMAGE. PROFESSOR SEWARD IS THERE NOW.

I OFFERED MY HELP, BUT HE WAS MOST PUT OUT BY THE IDEA. HE SEEMED MORE ANXIOUS THAT I CHECK ON MISS BOYD AND THE OTHERS.

BUT SINCE SHE'S ALREADY IN YOUR CARE...

NO, PLEASE!

PLEASE WOULD YOU STAY A WHILE DOCTOR? SHE IS OVER THE WORST AND IF THE PROFESSOR'S ALONE.

I'LL BE GLAD TO STAY. AFTER HER DREADFUL ORDEAL, I'M SURE THE YOUNG LADY WOULD BENEFIT FROM MY ATTENTION.

SIR, I CAN'T BEGIN TO THANK YOU.

NONSENSE. YOU MUST GO WHERE YOU ARE NEEDED. YOUR FIANCEE IS IN CAPABLE HANDS.

I GUARANTEE THAT WITHIN THE HOUR SHE WILL BE FULLY RECOVERED.

PROFESSOR SEWARD?

IN HEAVEN'S **NAME**, SIR!

IF YOU WERE TRYING TO FRIGHTEN ME OUT OF MY SKIN, YOU VERY NEARLY **SUCCEEDED**...

WHAT **HAPPENED** TO HER?

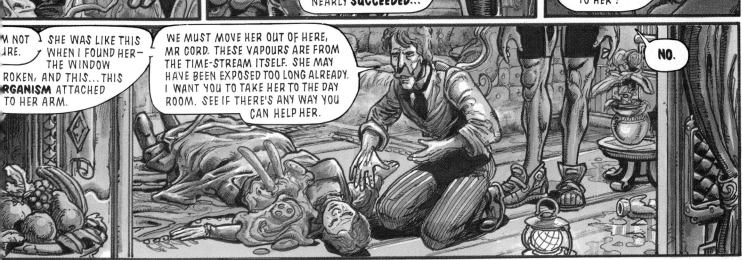

M NOT URE.

SHE WAS LIKE THIS WHEN I FOUND HER—THE WINDOW ROKEN, AND THIS...THIS RGANISM ATTACHED TO HER ARM.

WE MUST MOVE HER OUT OF HERE, MR CORD. THESE VAPOURS ARE FROM THE TIME-STREAM ITSELF. SHE MAY HAVE BEEN EXPOSED TOO LONG ALREADY. I WANT YOU TO TAKE HER TO THE DAY ROOM. SEE IF THERE'S ANY WAY YOU CAN HELP HER.

NO.

WANT **YOU** TO TAKE HER TO THE AY ROOM. I'VE GOT THIS **MESS** TO SORT OUT.

PROFESSOR SEWARD? IS THAT YOU?

OH, THANK HEAVENS YOU'RE HERE.

I THOUGHT I WAS GOING TO BE TRAPPED IN THIS DAMNED MIST FOR EVER. I CAN'T HAVE COME MORE THAN TWENTY YARDS, YET IT SEEMS TO HAVE TAKEN ME HOURS.

REALLY?
NOW THAT **IS**
INTERESTING.

LOOK, NEVER MIND THAT.
THERE ARE PEOPLE IN THE
LAST TWO CARRIAGES,
AND THE MIST'S HEADING
STRAIGHT TOWARDS
THEM...

YOU TWO TAKE THE COOK BACK TO THE
DAY ROOM. I'M GOING INTO THE
SERVANTS' QUARTERS. I'LL GET OUT
WHOEVER I CAN, THEN SEAL OFF
THE REAR OF THE TRAIN.

YOU CAN'T BE **SERIOUS**...?
MR CORD, THERE ARE
THINGS IN THERE—TERRIBLE
INHUMAN THINGS...

DON'T WORRY ABOUT ME. JUST
GET MRS HARRIS OUT OF HERE.

NOW GO ON.

GO ON!

I PRESENT THEE, O GREAT **SUCCOR BENOTH**, CHIEF OF THE EUNUCHS, THIS BODY AS THE PUREST I CAN OBTAIN...

I OFFER IT, O GRAND AND OMNIPOTENT ADONAY, ELIOM, ARIEL AND JEHOVAM, WITH MY WHOLE SOUL AND MY WHOLE HEART.

VOUCHSAFE TO RECEIVE IT AS AN ACCEPTABLE HOLOCAUST.

WITH THIS KNIFE, BORNE OF MY FLESH, I DIVIDE HER BODY INTO FIVE.

WITH THIS KNIFE, BLESSED IN THY NAME, I CUT THE KEYS IN THE SIGNS OF CONJURATION AND UNBINDING.

IN THESE SIGNS, THOSE OF THE INFERNAL PENTAGRAM AND THE FIVE KEYS OF SOLOMON, I WILL OPEN WIDE THE GATES TO THE ABYSS...

HERE IS THE FIRST KEY, CUT OF HER FLESH, MADE IN THE SIGN OF ASTAROTH...

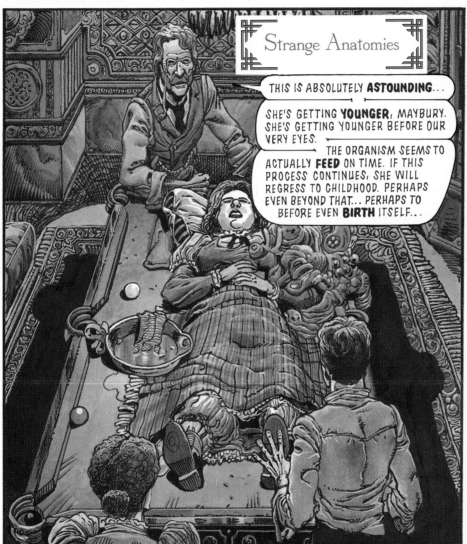

Strange Anatomies

THIS IS ABSOLUTELY **ASTOUNDING**...

SHE'S GETTING **YOUNGER**, MAYBURY. SHE'S GETTING YOUNGER BEFORE OUR VERY EYES.

THE ORGANISM SEEMS TO ACTUALLY **FEED** ON TIME. IF THIS PROCESS CONTINUES, SHE WILL REGRESS TO CHILDHOOD. PERHAPS EVEN BEYOND THAT... PERHAPS TO BEFORE EVEN **BIRTH** ITSELF...

BUT DON'T YOU SEE WHAT THIS **MEANS**, FATHER?

THE MESSAGE, THE WARNING I RECEIVED AT THE SEANCE — THE BLOOD, THE **THING** OUTSIDE, TRYING TO GET IN...

IT'S COMING **TRUE**.

SO... THIS IS WHERE THE **INSOMNIACS** GATHER, IS IT?

MR WINWOOD! **YOU** WERE AT THE SEANCE... TELL MY FATHER WHAT HAPPENED...

I DON'T KNOW WHAT YOU **MEAN**, MY DEAR...

THE **BLOOD!** THAT **DREADFUL** SPECTRE!

THE FEELING THAT SOMETHING WAS **WATCHING** US. SOMETHING OLD AND WISE...

SOMETHING UNSPEAKABLY **EVIL**.

MARY!

THWUMP!

I WILL **NOT** HAVE YOU ABUSING MY GUESTS IN THIS WAY. THIS FOOLISHNESS MUST **STOP**.

YOU NEVER HAD TIME FOR ME, DID YOU, FATHER? EVEN WHEN MOTHER DIED, EVEN **THEN**, YOU WERE TOO BUSY FOR ME.

VERY WELL, I'LL GO TO DOCTOR CULVER. AT LEAST, **HE'LL** LISTEN TO ME.

IT'S MORE THAN **YOU** EVER DID, FATHER.

JUST EXACTLY HOW FAR BACK **ARE** WE, OLD BOY?

I'M NOT SURE. AT A GUESS, I'D SAY ABOUT TEN THOUSAND MILLION YEARS, BUT THE TIME GAUGE IS PLAYING UP AGAIN.

DAMN THIS THING...

I THINK IT'S THE EXTERNAL PRESSURE WE SHOULD BE WORRYING ABOUT, VERNON.

WE'VE ALREADY HAD ONE BLOW-OUT. I REALLY DON'T THINK WE COULD SURVIVE ANOTHER...

BUT WE'RE SO **NEAR**. WE'RE ON THE **FINAL** THRESHOLD, ON THE VERY **CUSP** OF CREATION ITSELF...

WE CAN'T **POSSIBLY** STOP NOW.

MY DEAR CHAP, THAT'S THE **FARTHEST** THING FROM MY MIND. I WANT US TO COMPLETE THIS JOURNEY JUST AS MUCH AS **YOU**. BUT IN ONE **PIECE**, THAT'S ALL...

YOU'RE RIGHT, OF COURSE.

I'LL GO AHEAD TO THE ENGINE ROOM. IF THERE'S NO CHANGE IN THE TIME STREAM, I'LL START REDUCING OUR SPEED...

I SHOULDN'T BE LONG.

FOUL~PLAY

CHARLOTTE?

DOCTOR CULVER?

ARE YOU AWAKE?

AND THERE'S RED ON THE TRAIN

(ON THE WINDOW THE FLOOR)

(THE SEATS AND THE CEILING)

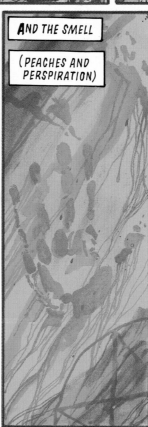

AND THE SMELL

(PEACHES AND PERSPIRATION)

AND THERE'S RED ON THE TRAIN

THERE'S RED ON THE TRAIN

THERE'S RED ON THE WINDOW, THE FLOOR, THE SEATS AND

i KNEW a mary once... i KNEW a mary twice

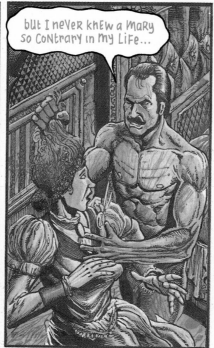

but I never knew a mary so contrary in my life...

WELL...? HOW SHALL WE PASS THE TIME?

Prof Vernon Seward

Lady Jocelyn Barrett-Gould & Lord Cecil Barrett-Gould (vinculum matrimonii)

Major Gordon Lyttelton

Sir Charles Langham
aegri somnia

Miss Charlotte Boyd
deceased

Miss Mary Seward & Dr Montague Culver
in flagrante delicto

Max Winwood
vitam regit fortuna non sapienta

Donald Maybury

Ishmael Cord
nil carborundum

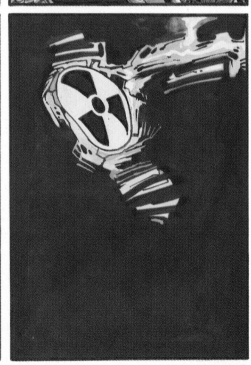

"SOMEHOW — THROUGH DREAMS, A PSI-LINK, CHAOS MAGIC — IT MADE CONTACT WITH THE GOOD DOCTOR. IT **CHANGED** HIM, SENDING HIM OUT TO HACK HIS WAY THROUGH THE BACK STREETS OF **WHITECHAPEL**..."

"OF COURSE, IT WASN'T ANY **ORDINARY** MURDER SPREE.

"EACH VICTIM FORMED ONE POINT OF A **CALVARY CROSS**, AN OCCULT SYMBOL DESIGNED TO OPEN A DOOR BETWEEN SPACETIME AND THE COREZONE... BETWEEN **YOUR** REALITY AND **THE ISCARIOT**.

"BUT THE PROCESS COULD ONLY GO SO F. THE ISCARIOT WAS **TOO** FAR AWAY, THE SACRIFICES **TOO** SMALL. IT WAS LIKE WHISPERING TO SOMEONE IN ANOTHER ROOM. SO CULVER HAD TO MOVE **NEARER**

"HE HELPED FINANCE SEWARD'S EXPERIMENTS, THREW IN THE ODD **SHRED** OF INFORMATION... ALL THE TIME WAITING TO COMPLETE THE CIRCLE.

"A FEW MINUTES AGO HE MADE HIS LAST SACRIFICE.

"THE CIRCLE WAS CLOSED. THE TUMBLERS CLICKED. THE DOOR **OPENED**... AND WE BROKE THROUGH INTO THE COREZONE."

LEAVING A DAMN GREAT **HOLE** BEHIND US...

THE ISCARIOT'S ALREADY LEAKING OUT, TRICKLING INTO SPACETIME LIKE WATER FROM A LEAKY BUCKET.

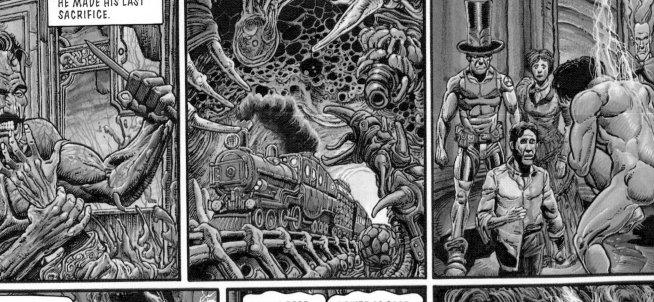

WE HAVE TO PUT A STOP TO IT, ONCE AND FOR ALL.

...TOO...IT'S TOO...LATE...

YOU'RE DEAD... YOU'RE AS GOOD AS DEAD...

EVERY ON OF YOU.

DONALD?
IT'S MARY.

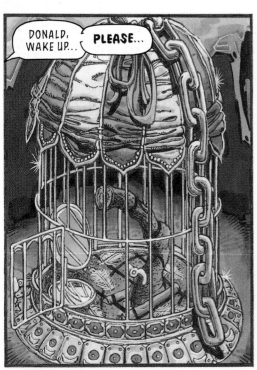

DONALD,
WAKE UP... PLEASE...

YOU CAN'T GO TO
SLEEP NOW. NOT
HERE...

LOOK, YOUR
CLOTHES ARE ALL
WET...

THEY'RE
COVERED
IN...

WHAT IS IT?
WHAT ON EARTH
HAPPENED?

WE WERE PREPARING
FOR BED AND SUDDENLY
THERE WAS THE MOST...

THERE'S BEEN AN
ACCIDENT,
HASN'T THERE?

Wounds are Licked

LADY, YOU DON'T KNOW THE **HALF** OF IT.

OH MY LORD...

HERE **ARE** WE? [W]HAT ARE WE [D]OING HERE?

[W]HO **ARE** YOU PEOPLE?

JUDAS **PRIEST**...

DON'T SAY WE'RE GONNA HAVE TO GO THROUGH ALL **THAT** AGAIN...

IT...IT'S CULVER. DOCTOR CULVER. HE KILLED CH-CH-CHARLOTTE.

THE ENTITY, THE **THING** WE FELT AT THE SEANCE... IT WAS **HIM**.

MARY!
OH, THANK HEAVENS YOU'RE SAFE!

PITY 三HIC三... WE WEREN'T **ALL** SO DAMNED **LUCKY!**

WHAT **HAPPENED,** VERNON?

I'M NOT SURE. THERE WAS SOMETHING— **SOMEONE** — ON THE LINE. I TRIED TO PUT ON THE BRAKES BUT...

ISHMAEL. A WORD...

THESE PEOPLE ARE JOLLY DISTRAUGHT. IT LOOKS LIKE I'VE GOT A SPOT OF EXPLAINING TO DO...

WHY DON'T **YOU** HAVE A QUICK SCOUT AROUND WHILE I'M DOING IT?

MAX, WE'RE IN THE MIDDLE OF THE **COREZONE,** NOT **MARKS & SPENCERS.**

THIS IS UNKNOWN TERRITORY. THERE COULD BE **ANYTHING** OUT THERE.

OH, COME **ON**... WHATEVER HAPPENED TO YOUR SENSE OF **ADVENTURE?**

I TRADED IT IN FOR A SET OF BUBBLE-GUM CARDS.

LOOK, YOU WANTED TO GIVE CULVER HIS JUST DESERTS, DIDN'T YOU? WELL, WHY DON'T YOU FINISH HIM **OFF?**

ONCE AND FOR ALL.

CALL IT A LUCKY GUESS, IF Y□ WANT, BUT SOMETHING TELL□ ME HE WENT **THAT** WAY...

That's it. Hurt me. Strip the flesh from my bones.

Kill me. Come on.

Give it your best shot...

He's going to take your arms. Those strong blue arms. You'll never fly the trapeze again...

You'll...

Aaaak!

What are you doing? What do you think you're doing?

This is for Charlotte.

no! Please, God, don't...

NaaUUgHHHHH

And in its hall of flesh, the Iscariot tasted blood and smiled.

KILLING TIME

WINWOOD AND CORD IN — AN INDIGO PRIME STORY

BY SMITH AND WESTON — PART: NINE

The House That Jack Built

SO THIS IS WHAT IT COMES TO.

FINALLY.

BRITTLE CORAL BRANCHES AS SHARP AS SHARP GLASS.

A SOUR WIND STRAGGLING THROUGH AN UNFINISHED LANDSCAPE.

BABIES SCREAMING IN AN EMPTY ROOM, CRYING FOR MOTHERS THEY NEVER HAD.

THIS IS WHERE IT ALL LEADS.

HERE.

NOW.

AND SOMETHING BAD'S GOING TO HAPPEN BUT HE DOESN'T KNOW WHAT.

ISHMAEL'S FINGERS START TO ITCH.

LOOK WHAT DADDY'S GOT FOR YOU...

LOOK.

DADDY'S GOT A PRETTY PRESENT FOR BABY. A PRETTY LITTLE PRESENT, JUST FOR BABY-KINS.

WHY DON'T WE SING THE 'THANK-YOU' SONG FOR DADDY?

AND:

AND:

MAJOR LYTTELTON IS TRAPPED, BURIED UNDER AN AVALANCHE OF WHISKERS AND FLOPPY EARS AND WET SNUFFLY NOSES.

AFTER A FEW MINUTES OF CAREFUL GROOMING, THE RABBITS START TO BURROW.

WHITE PAWS TURNING PINK.

MARY'S TEETH ARE CHATTERING. LIKE CASTANETS. LIKE THE RATTLE OF TYPEWRITER KEYS.

GRINDING TEETH AND SPITTLE IN THE AIR.

IF SHE TRIES TO PUSH THEM AWAY THEY SNAP AT HER, SO SHE SITS STILL, WISHING THEY'LL GO AWAY.

THE TEETH START TO SNIGGER...

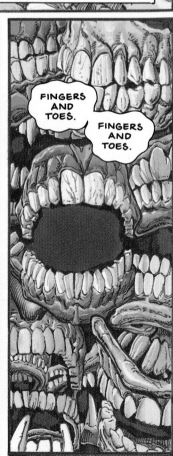

FINGERS AND TOES.

FINGERS AND TOES.

CHOM

CHOM

CHOM

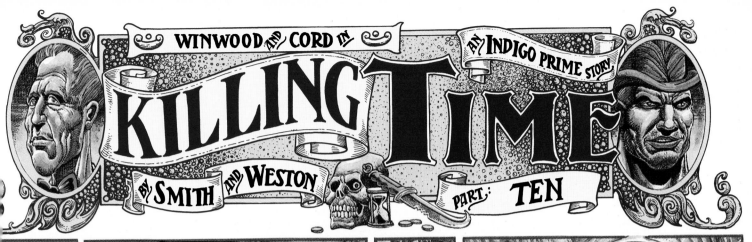

WINWOOD AND CORD IN
AN INDIGO PRIME STORY
KILLING TIME
BY SMITH AND WESTON
PART: TEN

MUH... AUHR...
NO MORE...

YOU BLACKGUARD!

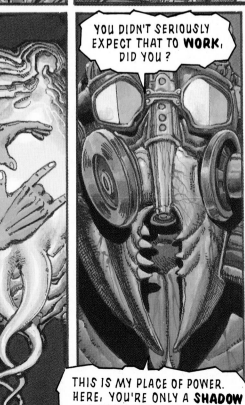

THIS IS MY PLACE OF POWER. HERE, YOU'RE ONLY A SHADOW OF YOUR REAL SELF.

YOU DIDN'T SERIOUSLY EXPECT THAT TO WORK, DID YOU?

PULL YOURSELF TOGETHER. YOU'RE AN EMBARRASSMENT TO YOUR SPECIES.

DRY YOUR EYES AND I'LL LET THE BLUE BOY DOWN.

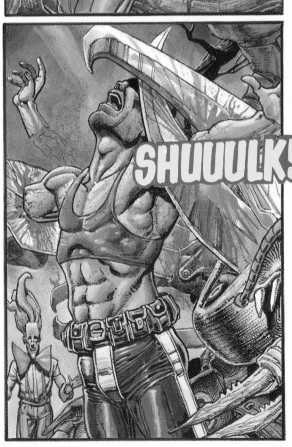

SHUUULK!

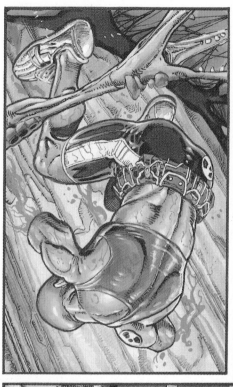

AAAA

AUH
AAA
AHH

WHY ARE YOU DOING THIS?

YOU PUT ME HERE, WINWOOD. YOU AND YOUR COLLEAGUES. LOCKED IN THIS BLIND WHITE CAGE FOR CENTURIES.

DID YOU REALLY THINK IT COULD **CONTAIN** ME?

"OVER THE YEARS I GREW LEAN, MY BODY SHRIVELLING AWAY, **ACRES** OF FLESH WASTING TO **NOTHING**.

"BUT MY **MIND**...

"I LEARNED TO SLIP BETWEEN THE BARS, SENDING MY MIND FLUTTERING OUT THROUGH HISTORY.

"MOVING THE LITTLE PEOPLE FROM HERE TO THERE, STAGING WARS AND FAMINES...

"SOWING MY SEED ACROSS THE FUTURE...

"BUT, AS WITH ALL THINGS, REALITY HAD ITS **FLAWS**.

"SO MUCH **SLOVENLINESS**, SO MANY UNTIDY MINDS, CLUTTERED WITH RUBBLE AND BRIC-A-BRAC.

"SO I SOUGHT TO **RE-MAKE** THE WORLD IN MY OWN IMAGE.

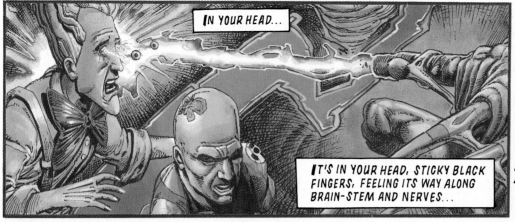

IN YOUR HEAD...

IT'S IN YOUR HEAD, STICKY BLACK FINGERS, FEELING ITS WAY ALONG BRAIN-STEM AND NERVES...

NOW... WHY DON'T YOU GO FIRST?

FORGET THAT

BUT THE PAIN

THINK ABOUT THE BIRD, WINGS FLUTTERING, ITS TINY HEARTBEAT.

NOW DOUBLE IT (CUT AND SPLICE), FOLD TIME BACK ON ITSELF AND DOUBLE IT.

TAKE THE BIRD

OH GODDD

TAKE THE BIRD A SECOND INTO THE PAST.

IT HURRRTTS

(TWO BIRDS)

TAKE THOSE TWO ANOTHER SECOND INTO THE PAST.

(FOUR)

AND AGAIN

(EIGHT)

AND AGAIN

(SIXTEEN)

AND AGAIN

(THIRTY-TWO)

AND AGAIN

AND AGAIN

AND AGAIN

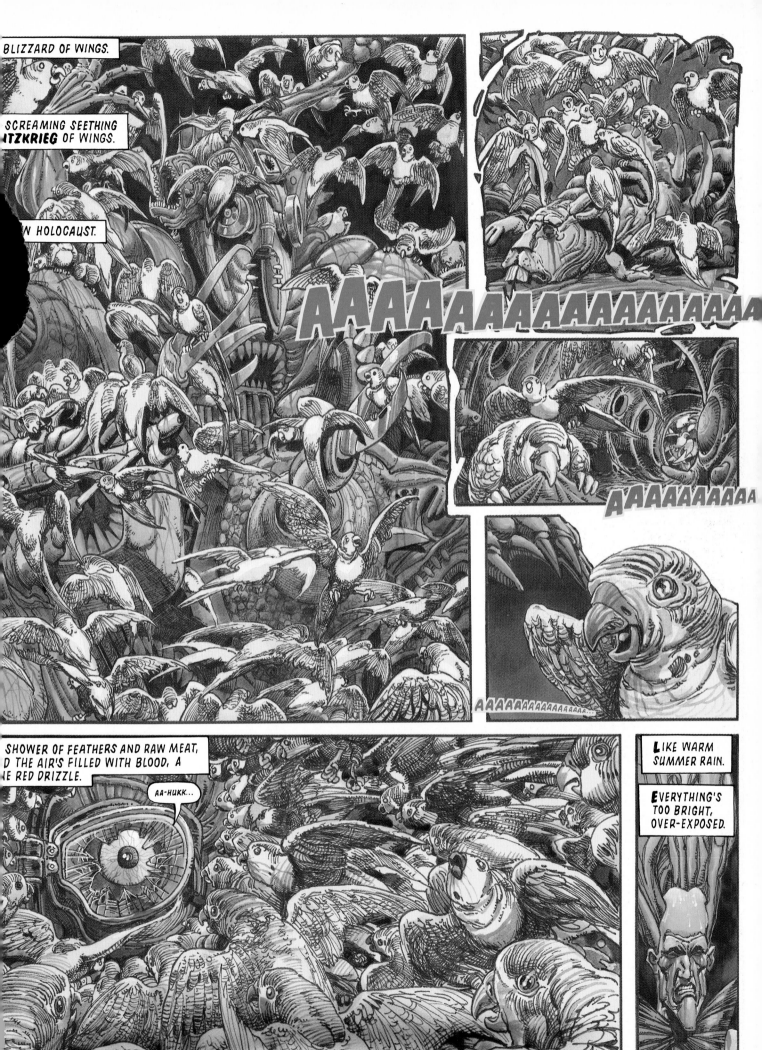

THE CAGE IS COLLAPSING AROUND US, SPACE AND TIME FOLDING IN ON ITSELF LIKE A CHEAP PAPER BOX.

THE PULL OF GRAVITY, DEEP IN THE BONES.

AND OH, THE SOUND... LIKE THE RUSHING OF THE SEA, LIKE A HURRICANE.

IT'S ALL GOING TO PIECES.

MAX?

MAX, I'M SCARED.

HOLD MY HAND. MAX, PLEASE...WILL YOU HOLD MY HAND?

IT'S ALL RIGHT. I'M HERE. I'M HOLDING YOUR HAND. I'M HOLDING IT NOW.

I CAN FEEL IT. OH, THANK YOU. I CAN FEEL IT...

DON'T WORRY ABOUT A THING. JUST CLOSE YOUR EYES AND HOLD ON TIGHT. WE'RE GOING HOME.

MAX? ARE WE GOING HOME?

YES.

ANY MINUTE NOW. YOU'LL SEE.

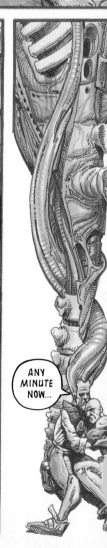

ANY MINUTE NOW...